D1613708

rg

SPECTACULAR SPACE SCIENCE

Exploring
COMETS,
ASTEROIDS,
AND OTHER OBJECTS IN SPACE

Nancy Dickmann

rosen publishing's
rosen
central

New York

Published in 2016 by The Rosen Publishing Group, Inc.
29 East 21st Street
New York, NY 10010

Produced for Rosen by Calcium
Editors for Calcium: Sarah Eason and Jennifer Sanderson
Designer: Greg Tucker
Consultant: David Hawksett

Photo credits: Cover courtesy of NASA; p. 4 © Dreamstime/Laurence Romaric; p. 5 courtesy of NASA/ JPL; p. 6 courtesy of Wikimedia Commons/Brown University Library; p. 7 courtesy of Wikimedia Commons/ Edmund Weiß; p. 8 courtesy of Wikimedia Commons/http://www.phys.uu.nl/~vgent/astrology/newton. htm; p. 9 courtesy of Wikimedia Commons/AntMan6104; p. 11 courtesy of Wikimedia Commons/Hans Bernhard; p. 12 courtesy of NASA/Halley Multicolor Camera Team/Giotto Project/ESA; p. 13 courtesy of ESA; p. 14 bottom courtesy of NASA/JPL; pp. 14–15 courtesy of NASA; p. 16 courtesy of NASA/JPL/ UMD/Pat Rawlings; p. 17 top courtesy of ESA/Rosetta/MPS for OSIRIS Team MPS/UPD/LAM/IAA/SSO/ INTA/UPM/DASP/IDA; p. 17 bottom courtesy of ESA ESA/Rosetta/NAVCAM; p. 19 © Shutterstock/Andrea Danti; p. 20 courtesy of Wikimedia Commons/NASA/JPL; p. 21 courtesy of NASA/Ed Schilling; p. 22 courtesy of NASA; p. 23 courtesy of NASA/JPL-Caltech/UCLA/MPS/DLR/IDA; p. 24 courtesy of Wikimedia Commons/Vokrug Sveta; p. 25 © Shutterstock/John A Davis; p. 26 © Shutterstock/fabiodevilla; p. 27 © Dreamstime/Pytyczech; p. 28 courtesy of Wikimedia Commons; p. 29 © Dreamstime/Walter Arce; pp. 30–31 © Dreamstime/Barold; p. 32 courtesy of NASA/JPL-Caltech; p. 33 courtesy of NASA/JPL/Space Science Institute; p. 35 courtesy of NASA/ESA/G. Bacon (STScI); p. 36 courtesy of Wikimedia Commons/ Dutch National Archives; p. 37 courtesy of NASA/JPL/USGS; p. 38 © Shutterstock/liquid studios; p. 39 © Shutterstock/solarseven; p. 40 courtesy of NASA; p. 41 courtesy of NASA/Eric James; p. 42 © Dreamstime/Jankaliciak; p. 43 © Shutterstock/Oleksiy Mark; p. 44 courtesy of NASA; p. 45 courtesy of NASA/Goddard/University of Arizona.

Library of Congress Cataloging-in-Publication Data

Dickmann, Nancy, author.
Exploring comets, asteroids, and other objects in space/Nancy Dickmann.—First edition.
    pages cm.—(Spectacular space science)
Includes bibliographical references and index.
ISBN 978-1-4994-3637-2 (library bound)—ISBN 978-1-4994-3639-6 (pbk.)—
ISBN 978-1-4994-3640-2 (6-pack)
1. Space sciences—Juvenile literature. 2. Comets—Juvenile literature. 3. Asteroids—Juvenile literature. 4. Meteors—Juvenile literature. 5. Outer space—Exploration—Juvenile literature. I. Title.
QB500.22.D53 2016
523—dc23
                                                                    2014047233

Manufactured in the United States of America

CONTENTS

Chapter One

THE HIDDEN SOLAR SYSTEM

Think of the solar system, and what do you picture? There is the sun at the center, of course, shining brightly. Surrounding it are Earth and the other seven planets, each orbiting the sun in its own path. Is that it? You may have heard about Pluto, whose orbit crosses that of Neptune and used to be considered a planet but is now classified as a dwarf planet. What else could there be in our solar system?

It turns out that there is a lot more to the solar system than just a star and eight planets. The solar system includes everything that is held in orbit by the sun's gravity. The planets are the biggest objects in the solar system but there are trillions of smaller objects. These include more than 146 moons orbiting the planets, five recognized dwarf planets, and more than 150 million asteroids.

The sun is at the center of the solar system. It produces energy in the form of heat, light, and other radiation.

However, even that is only scratching the surface. Comets swoop in from the outer reaches of the solar system, making a long loop around the sun before disappearing back to where they came from. A largely unexplored region called the Kuiper Belt lies outside the orbit of Neptune and is home to trillions of objects. Many of them are probably big enough to be classified as dwarf planets, once more is known about them. Then there are also the centaurs and trojans. Centaurs are small solar system bodies with a semi-major axis between those of the outer planets. A trojan is a space body that shares an orbit with a planet or larger moon.

Ganymede is bigger than Mercury, but still not classed as a planet. This is because it orbits Jupiter, making it a moon.

WHERE DOES THE SOLAR SYSTEM END?

The solar system goes much farther than the most outlying planet, Neptune, but just how big it is depends on how you define it. The heliopause marks the boundary of the heliosphere, an area filled with solar magnetic fields and solar winds. However, beyond that is the Oort Cloud, an enormous collection of icy comets. They are outside the heliosphere but still affected by the sun's gravity, so they are usually considered to be part of the solar system.

Early Sightings

Long before telescopes were invented, people studied the skies. They tracked the movements of the sun, moon, and stars, as well as those planets that could be seen with the naked eye: Mercury, Venus, Mars, Jupiter, and Saturn. Although the planets look a lot like stars when seen from Earth, early astronomers could tell that they were different because of their movements over the course of a year.

Before electric light affected our view of the skies, there would have been thousands of stars visible on a clear night. However, most of the other objects in the solar system are too small and too far away to be seen without a telescope. Moons circling other planets, asteroids, and Kuiper Belt objects (KBOs) were completely unknown to ancient peoples.

However, a few of our solar system neighbors did make appearances from time to time, and when they showed up, they really made a splash! When some comets approach Earth on their way to the sun, they can be seen streaking brightly across the sky, their long tails streaming out behind them. Many people interpreted comets as a sign that something bad would happen soon: the death of a king, war, or natural disasters, for example.

In 1853, a bright comet became visible to the naked eye, causing a sensation in Paris and other cities.

STONES FROM HEAVEN

Meteors sometimes fall to Earth in the form of stones that we call meteorites. For thousands of years, people have found and collected these stones. They must have seen some of them fall from the sky, an experience that would have been both mysterious and terrifying. Many meteorites have been found in contexts that suggest that they were worshipped, or believed to have special powers.

The Leonid meteor shower of 1833 was particularly spectacular. It is estimated that more than 100,000 meteors were seen in a single hour!

The other objects that were often seen were meteors, sometimes called "shooting stars." These are much more common than comets, and if you happen to be looking in the right place at the right time, you can see one most nights. Sometimes they come in groups, called a meteor shower, and many people thought they brought good luck. One culture believed that seeing one meteor would bring good fortune, but three in one night would bring death!

7

More than Just Planets

By the eighteenth century, there was enough data for astronomers and mathematicians to study patterns in comets. In 1705, Edmond Halley (1656–1742) analyzed historical sightings of twenty-three different comets, according to Newton's Laws of Motion. He noticed that three of them (from 1531, 1607, and 1682), had very similar paths. He theorized that they must have all been the same comet, and predicted that it would return in 1758 or 1759. He was right! The comet is now called Halley's Comet in his honor.

During that period, telescopes were revolutionizing the study of the solar system. Some mathematicians noticed that the distance of the planets from the sun seemed to form a pattern. As you move out from Mercury, the gap between the planets increases at a regular rate. The six known planets fit this pattern very neatly, with one exception: there was a huge gap between Mars and Jupiter, with just the right amount of space for a missing planet in between. When Uranus was discovered in 1781, it also fit neatly into the pattern, encouraging scientists to believe that there really was a planet between Mars and Jupiter!

Edmond Halley died in 1742, so he did not live to see his prediction about the comet proved right.

By the end of the century, a group of astronomers had formed a team to search for the missing planet using an observatory in Germany. They called themselves the "Celestial Police." An Italian astronomer, Giuseppe Piazzi (1746–1826), thought he beat them to it when he discovered Ceres in 1801. Piazzi and other scientists considered it a planet, however, Ceres was fewer than six hundred miles (966 kilometers) across—even the smallest planet, Mercury, is more than three thousand miles (4,828 km) across. After half a century of "planet" status, during which other objects even smaller than Ceres were discovered, Ceres was reclassified as an asteroid.

BODE'S LAW BUSTED

The pattern of planets was called Bode's Law, and most scientists now believe that it is just a coincidence, rather than a law of nature. When Neptune was discovered in 1846, its position went against Bode's Law. After years of searching, astronomers came to the conclusion that there was no single, large planet between Mars and Jupiter.

In Halley's day, many cities and universities had an observatory tower, such as this one in Palermo, Italy. Today, most major telescopes are set up far from cities and other sources of light pollution, which can distort the images scientists observe through telescopes.

Chapter Two

COMETS

Comets have inspired many fantastic stories and legends, but the truth behind them is fairly simple. They are small, icy objects, mostly between six and twenty-five miles (9.7 and 40 km) in diameter, and they heat up when they pass close to the sun. When this happens, some of a comet's icy center (called the nucleus) turns to gas, forming a thin atmosphere called a coma. The solar wind blows the coma material, which makes a comet's trademark tails. A comet's tails stream out for millions of miles.

Comets are found in the outer reaches of the solar system, in the Kuiper Belt, and the Oort Cloud. Many of these icy lumps will never leave their home but others have their orbits disturbed (usually by the gravity of another object) and are sent on a new path. Those that move toward the sun begin to vaporize in the warmer areas of the inner solar system, which creates the coma and tails.

Unlike planets, comets traveling around the sun do not follow a round orbit. Instead, they travel in very long, thin loops. Once they pass the sun they do not continue across to the other side of the solar system; instead, they loop back around and return to where they came from. Short-period comets, like Halley's Comet, mainly come from the Kuiper Belt and complete an orbit in fewer than two hundred years. Long-period comets come from the Oort Cloud and can take thirty million years to make a trip around the sun!

COMET THEORIES

In the seventeenth century, Isaac Newton (1643–1727) theorized that the tails of comets were streams of vapor emitted by their bodies and ignited by the sun. In the next century, Immanuel Kant (1724–1804) suggested that the comets themselves were made of a substance that vaporized to form the tail. In 1950, Fred Whipple (1906–2004) correctly proposed that comets are mainly icy objects containing some dust and rock, like a dirty snowball.

A comet has two tails: one made of gas and one made of dust. The gas tail is pushed away from the sun, no matter in which direction the comet is traveling.

Studying Halley's Comet

Probably the most famous comet is Halley's Comet, a short-period comet that is visible from Earth every seventy-five to seventy-six years. It is the first comet that was recognized to be periodic; that is, to have a regularly timed orbit. It is easily seen by the naked eye when it approaches Earth, and its appearances were recorded throughout history, although people at the time did not realize that it was the same comet returning.

When Halley's Comet appeared in 1910, the first-ever photographs of it were taken. Astronomers were also able to take some readings and learn more about what it was made of. On its next appearance in 1986, conditions for viewing it from Earth were poor: it did not make a very close approach, and light pollution caused by electricity (which was not such a problem in 1910) kept many people from being able to see it.

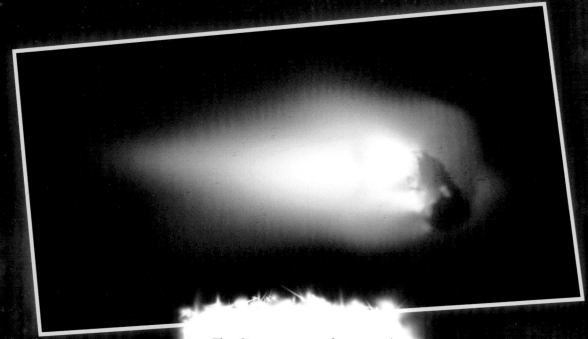

The Giotto spacecraft snapped this photograph of the nucleus of Halley's Comet in 1986.

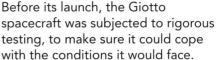

Before its launch, the Giotto spacecraft was subjected to rigorous testing, to make sure it could cope with the conditions it would face.

However, scientists were able to use technology to make the most of Halley's approach. A French/Soviet probe sent back the first-ever image of its nucleus. The European Space Agency (ESA) launched the Giotto probe, which made the closest pass to the nucleus and sent back even better photographs. Two Japanese probes also studied the comet. The International Cometary Explorer (ICE) spacecraft passed through the comet's tail, although it never got very close to the comet itself. Two space shuttle missions from the National Aeronautics and Space Administration (NASA) were planned to study the comet, but they were canceled after the Challenger space shuttle exploded earlier that year. With improvements in technology, who knows what we might be able to learn when the comet returns in 2061?

HISTORICAL SIGHTINGS

A Chinese historian recorded a comet as far back as 240 BCE, a year when Halley would have been visible. Archaeologists have found records of its next two appearances on Babylonian tablets, and historians from many cultures recorded the next few visits. When it appeared again in 1066 it was seen as an omen that predicted the victory of William the Conqueror over the English king.

13

Later Missions

Giotto found that Halley's nucleus was dark, probably because of a thick layer of dust. The material it was releasing was mainly water, with smaller amounts of carbon monoxide, methane, and ammonia. Studying Halley's Comet in 1986 was just the start, and later probes have increased our knowledge of comets. After studying Halley's Comet, Giotto remained in orbit in hibernation mode for more than four years. It was "woken up" in 1990 to get into position for a meeting with Comet Grigg-Skjellerup (a much older comet) in 1992.

NASA's Deep Space 1 spacecraft was launched in 1998. It was mainly designed as a test run for several new technologies, including an ion drive in place of a traditional rocket engine. However, one of its missions was an encounter with Comet Borrelly. Deep Space 1 was able to send back detailed photographs of the comet's surface that were much clearer than Giotto's photographs of Halley's Comet.

This illustration shows Deep Space 1 using its ion drive to approach Comet Borrelly. The spacecraft also had software that allowed it to make its own navigation decisions.

COMET CRASH

In 1994, scientists had an opportunity to see the death of a comet. Shoemaker-Levy 9 had been discovered in orbit around Jupiter the year before. Comets can be "captured" by the gravity of larger objects, and this is probably what happened to Shoemaker-Levy 9. It had been torn into pieces by Jupiter's gravity, and from July 16 to July 22, 1994, the fragments of the comet smashed into Jupiter at about 134,000 miles per hour (215,650 km per hour).

This series of images, taken by the Stardust probe, shows comet Wild 2 as the spacecraft got closer and closer to it.

The Stardust probe was launched a year after Deep Space 1. It intercepted Wild 2 and approached as close as 147 miles (237 km) from the comet's nucleus, taking detailed photographs. Its most impressive achievement was collecting dust samples from the comet's coma, then returning these samples to Earth for scientists to analyze. The Sample Return Capsule parachuted safely to the ground in Utah on January 16, 2006. Stardust also approached the comet Tempel 1 in 2011.

Inside a Comet

When the sun first formed, it was surrounded by a flat, disc-shaped cloud of ice and dust. As this cloud rotated, the particles in it started sticking together and forming bigger and bigger lumps. Some of the lumps closer to the sun eventually became planets and asteroids, and the ones far from the sun became comets. Astronomers are interested in comets because they are like time capsules. Finding out what they are made of can show us what the solar system was like in its very early days.

In the 1990s, NASA designed a spacecraft to do just that. The Deep Impact mission was launched in 2005 on a course that would take it to intercept Tempel 1. Unlike previous probes such as Giotto and Stardust, which had only flown past and taken photographs, Deep Impact would release an impactor. The impactor used its thrusters to move itself into the path of the comet, and Tempel 1 then crashed into it at a speed of twenty-three thousand miles per hour (37,000 km per hour). The collision caused a crater five hundred feet (152 meters) across, and the Deep Impact spacecraft, three hundred miles (483 km) away, took photographs and other readings. Scientists were surprised to find that the comet contained more dust but less ice than they expected.

After the successful impact with Temple 1, the spacecraft still had plenty of fuel left, so the mission was renamed EPOXI and began studying planets outside the solar system, as well as making a flyby of Comet Hartley in 2010.

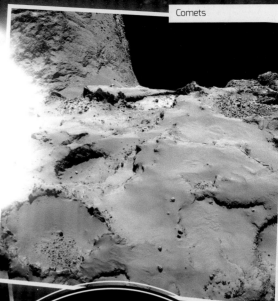

Right: Rosetta's images allowed scientists to choose different potential landing sites for Philae. Unfortunately, the lander bounced when it landed, missing the chosen sites.

Bottom: Rosetta took amazingly clear photographs of Comet 67P/Churyumov-Gerasimenko.

PHILAE

Rosetta carried a small lander called Philae. On November 12, 2014, Philae dropped to comet Churyumov-Gerasimenko's surface. It was a difficult landing, and Philae ended up in an area of deep shadow, which did not receive enough sunlight for its solar panels to recharge its batteries. However, it drilled into the surface and sent back data for more than fifty hours before falling silent.

ESA launched Rosetta in 2004 to study the comet Churyumov-Gerasimenko. In 2014, Rosetta successfully entered orbit around the comet. Over the course of its seventeen-month orbit, it studied the comet in detail, looking for signs of organic compounds—the building blocks of life. This evidence could prove the theory that long ago, comets crashing into Earth "seeded" it with organic molecules.

Chapter Three

ASTEROIDS

Asteroids are a little like very small planets. The smallest are the size of boulders, and the biggest ones are several hundred miles across. Most of them are found in the asteroid belt that lies between the orbits of Mars and Jupiter. Like comets, they were formed from the "leftovers" in the early days of the solar system. Most of them, especially the smaller ones, are lumpy and oddly shaped. Asteroids are different from comets in several ways. They orbit the sun in a path that is roughly circular, like a planet does, instead of a long, thin loop like a comet's orbit. They are mainly made of rock and metals, although some asteroids are now known to contain water ice. Their surface does not vaporize to give them a coma or a tail. Their surfaces also show craters where other objects have crashed into them.

Asteroids may be fairly close to Earth, but studying them is not the easiest job. Most of them are so small that even seen with the powerful Hubble Space Telescope, which can peer into distant galaxies, they appear only as fuzzy blobs. Although we do not have many clear photographs of asteroids, we have found a lot of asteroids —at least 500,000. Most of them have been found since 1980.

NASA's Wide-field Infrared Survey Explorer (WISE) was launched in 2009. This space telescope was designed to take infrared images of 99 percent of the sky. In its ten-month mission it took more than 1.5 million images—that is one every eleven seconds! It detected tens of thousands of new asteroids. One of its jobs was identifying asteroids and other objects orbiting close to Earth.

TROJANS

Not all asteroids are found in the asteroid belt. A particular type of asteroid, called a trojan, shares its orbit with a larger object, such as a planet. Trojans stay far enough away from the larger object to avoid crashing into it. There are two large clusters of trojans in the orbit of Jupiter, which were the first to be found. Since then, trojans have been found sharing the orbits of Mars, Neptune, Uranus, and even Earth.

An object must have a lot of mass for its gravity to be strong enough to pull it into a spherical shape. Most asteroids do not have enough mass, and as a result they are lumpy.

Landing on an Asteroid

We cannot see asteroids clearly through telescopes but we can still learn a little about what they are like. By studying the variation in an asteroid's brightness as it rotates, astronomers can make educated guesses about its shape. Its size can be estimated by measuring how much a star's light dims when an asteroid passes directly in front of it. However, the best way to study asteroids up close is to visit them.

Several space probes have been launched to study asteroids. The first probe to do an asteroid flyby was Galileo in 1991, on its way to study Jupiter. It took photographs of the asteroid Gaspra, as well as an unusual asteroid named Ida, which has its own moon, named Dactyl.

Galileo took this photograph of Ida, which is only about nineteen miles (31 km) across. Its moon, Dactyl, is much smaller—about one mile (1.6 km) across.

When the Hayabusa's sample reentry capsule fell to Earth, it created a streak in the sky, similar to a meteor.

NASA's Near Earth Asteroid Rendezvour (NEAR) mission was the first mission to orbit an asteroid. The NEAR Shoemaker probe, launched in February 1996, photographed Mathilde in 1997 and then entered orbit around Eros in 2000. It studied Eros from orbit for nearly a year, before landing on the asteroid's surface to study it further.

The Japanese Aerospace Exploration Agency (JAXA) launched the Hayabusa probe in 2003. The probe was equipped with a mini-lander called MINERVA, which failed to land on the asteroid's surface. However, samples were collected and analyzed when the probe returned to Earth in 2010. On December 3, 2014, the Hayabusa 2 was launched with the hope it would get samples that could shed light on the origins of the solar system. It is expected to reach its target in 2018.

MOONS OR ASTEROIDS?

The Mariner 9 probe took the first clear photographs of asteroid-like objects in 1971, twenty years before NEAR Shoemaker. However, the objects it photographed are better known as Deimos and Phobos—the two tiny, lumpy moons that orbit Mars. Most astronomers believe that these moons were originally asteroids that were captured by Mars's gravity. The Voyager probes took photographs of other solar system moons that are also probably captured asteroids.

A New Dawn

The asteroids studied by the early probes were all fairly small. NASA's Dawn probe, launched in 2007, focused on two of the big hitters of the asteroid belt: Vesta and Ceres. Vesta is more than three hundred miles (483 km) in diameter. Ceres is the biggest object in the asteroid belt, and it is no longer considered to be an asteroid but instead a dwarf planet, in the same category as Pluto.

NEW TECHNOLOGY

Dawn made use of an exciting new technology: the ion drive. This new type of engine uses charged particles to create thrust. Its fuel is a gas (often xenon), and it needs to carry much less fuel than a conventional rocket engine. The Japanese Hayabusa probe also successfully used an ion thruster.

Dawn's solar panels were folded up to fit inside the rocket that launched it. Once in space, they extended to capture solar energy and power the ion drive.

Vesta and Ceres are also considered protoplanets. When the solar system first formed, a huge cloud of dust swirled around the sun. Eventually the particles started to collide and stick together to form lumps. Once the lumps became big enough, they could attract even more particles with their gravity. They got larger and larger until they formed protoplanets. Some protoplanets eventually formed planets, and others stayed as they were. A planet's composition changes as it gets bigger, and heavier materials sink into its core. A protoplanet provides a better snapshot of what the early solar system was like.

Dawn successfully entered orbit around Vesta in 2011. It remained in orbit for about a year, taking photographs and other readings. It was able to estimate the size of Vesta's core and reveal evidence of ancient asteroid impacts. It is expected to reach Ceres in 2015 and remain in orbit.

More missions to asteroids are in the planning stages. Like JAXA's Hayabusa 2 probe, NASA has its own sample return mission, OSIRIS-REx, in development. NASA is also working on a plan to capture a near-Earth asteroid (NEA) and move it into orbit around the moon. It could then be studied in detail by astronauts, and eventually crashed into the moon.

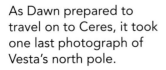

As Dawn prepared to travel on to Ceres, it took one last photograph of Vesta's north pole.

Impact?

There are a lot of objects in the solar system that orbit scarily close to Earth. Many of them are NEAs. You only have to look at the cratered surfaces of the moon or Mercury to know that objects in space have a habit of crashing into each other. We know that at several times in history, large objects have crashed into Earth. For example, many scientists believe that an asteroid six miles (9.7 km) across crashed into Earth about sixty-five million years ago, causing climate changes that contributed to the extinction of the dinosaurs.

An asteroid does not have to be very big to cause a lot of damage. In 1908, a huge explosion blasted a remote forest in northern Russia. There was no crater, but for miles around, the trees were scorched and knocked down. This explosion, now called the Tunguska Event, was felt hundreds of miles away. Many scientists believe that the explosion was caused by an asteroid or comet about one hundred feet (30.5 m) across, which exploded before it could impact the ground.

Space agencies regularly search for and monitor objects whose orbits take them close to Earth. They focus on those more than 0.6 miles (1 km) in diameter, which would be the most destructive if they crashed into Earth. An impact is unlikely in the near future, but it is best to be prepared!

The Tunguska explosion destroyed large areas of forest, but if it had landed in a large city, hundreds of thousands of people could have been killed.

WHAT COULD WE DO?

Several ideas have been proposed for dealing with an asteroid on a collision course with Earth. One method is to blow it up into smaller pieces, which will either be blown off course or burn up in the atmosphere. Some people have suggested using nuclear weapons to destroy asteroids. Another suggestion is to change the asteroid's course so that it misses Earth. Some scientists have proposed ramming them with a spacecraft or other objects to knock them off course. Another idea is to attach rocket engines to the asteroid, which could "drive" it out of harm's way.

This telescope in Arizona is one of many that tracks and studies NEAs.

25

Chapter Four

METEORS

If you look up at the sky on a clear night, you may be lucky enough to see a shooting star, a bright streak of light across the sky. The scientific name for a shooting star is a meteor, and meteors have nothing to do with stars! Little chunks of rock in space are called meteoroids. Occasionally they get close enough to Earth to enter our atmosphere. When they travel through the atmosphere, it creates friction, which makes the meteoroid so hot that it glows.

Many meteors burn up completely in the atmosphere. However, some make it through and land on Earth. When this happens, they are called meteorites. Over the centuries, people have found meteorites all over Earth. Antarctica is a particularly good place to find them. Ice provides a softer landing than rock, and meteorite rocks are easier to spot against a snowy background. Meteorites are a great way for scientists to study what other objects in   space are like without ever leaving Earth. In many cases they have been able to tell where a meteorite has come from, based on what it is made of.

For centuries, people made wishes on shooting stars, without knowing what they actually were.

We do not send spacecraft to visit or investigate meteoroids—they are just too small. They are not big enough to cause large-scale damage, so they are not tracked as diligently as asteroids are. However, they are the only type of object from space that regularly turns up practically on our doorstep!

The Hoba meteorite in Namibia in southwest Africa is the largest single meteorite ever found at about sixty tons (fifty-four metric tons). A farmer found it and dug it up from beneath the earth in 1920.

SMALL BUT QUICK

You would think that something visible high up in the sky would have to be fairly big, but a lot of meteors are quite small. In fact, most of the ones we see are caused by meteoroids smaller than a pebble, and some are no bigger than a grain of sand. Even these tiny objects can leave a trail several miles long because of their extremely high speed. Meteoroids can enter the atmosphere at anything from 25,000 to 160,000 miles per hour (40,250 to 257,500 km per hour).

Fireball!

Meteors can appear at any time of day or night, but the ones that happen during the day are usually impossible to see, because the sun is so bright. However, sometimes a meteoroid enters Earth's atmosphere and causes a spectacular fireball that is hard to miss, no matter how bright it is outside!

One of the most impressive fireballs in recent years was seen over Chelyabinsk, Russia, on February 15, 2013. A small asteroid estimated to be sixty-five feet (20 m) wide streaked across the sky, before exploding into thousands of smaller fragments at high altitude. The shock waves from the explosion shattered windows and damaged buildings, causing injuries from broken glass. Many pieces of the meteorite were recovered for study.

In 1992, thousands of people on the east coast of the United States saw a fireball race across the evening sky. It was a meteorite that eventually landed in Peekskill, New York, on top of a parked car. Many people caught it on film from different locations, and this helped scientists to calculate its flight path. A famous crater that was created by a meteor is Barringer Crater in Arizona. Scientists believe that it was created about fifty thousand years ago by a meteor that measured approximately 160 feet (49 m) across.

For a brief moment, the Chelyabinsk fireball shone more brightly than the sun.

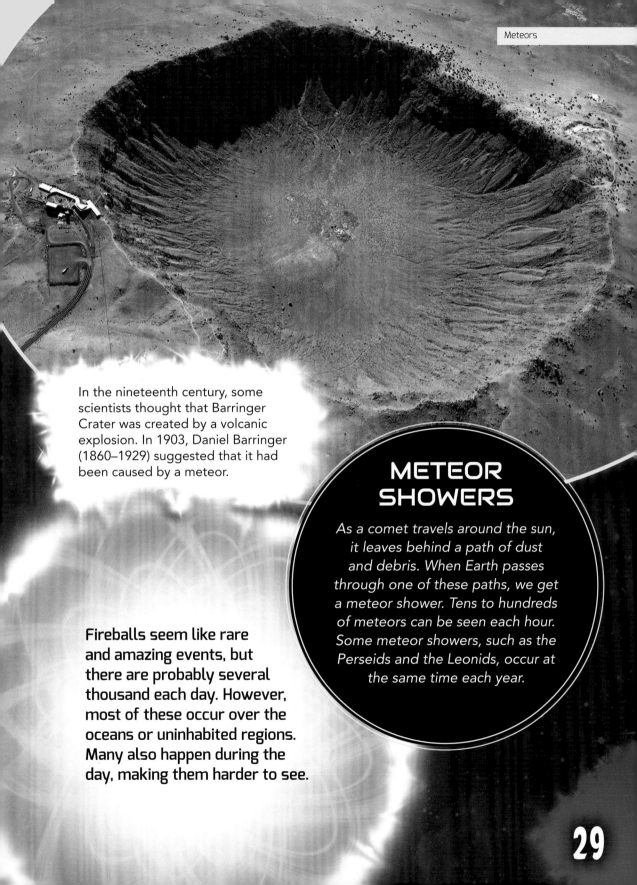

In the nineteenth century, some scientists thought that Barringer Crater was created by a volcanic explosion. In 1903, Daniel Barringer (1860–1929) suggested that it had been caused by a meteor.

METEOR SHOWERS

As a comet travels around the sun, it leaves behind a path of dust and debris. When Earth passes through one of these paths, we get a meteor shower. Tens to hundreds of meteors can be seen each hour. Some meteor showers, such as the Perseids and the Leonids, occur at the same time each year.

Fireballs seem like rare and amazing events, but there are probably several thousand each day. However, most of these occur over the oceans or uninhabited regions. Many also happen during the day, making them harder to see.

Learning From Meteorites

Finding a meteorite may feel like a once-in-a-lifetime event, but meteorites fall to Earth all the time. Scientists estimate that nearly forty-nine tons (forty-four metric tons) of meteorites land on Earth each day! Depending on where they came from, they can be very different in composition. Scientists divide meteorites into three main types: iron, stone, and stony-iron.

Most iron meteorites are 90 to 95 percent iron, with the remainder made up of nickel and trace elements. They are thought to be the cores of asteroids or long-gone planets. Stony-iron meteorites are made up of equal amounts of nickel-iron and stone. They are believed to have been formed at the core-mantle boundary of an asteroid or planet. Fewer than 2 percent of meteorites are stony-iron. Stony meteorites are the most common. They are believed to have come from the outer crust of other planets and asteroids.

The majority of meteorites that fall to Earth are the stone type, but many of the ones we find are irons. One reason for this is that irons are tougher and more likely to survive the fall. Meteorites do not just fall on Earth, either. In 2005, the Mars rover Opportunity found the first-ever meteorite on another planet: a metal meteorite about the size of a basketball. Mars has an extremely thin atmosphere, so meteoroids that hit it do not burn up as much as they do on Earth.

METEORITES FROM MARS

Nearly all meteorites that have been found come from asteroids. However, about 0.2 percent of them come from Mars or the moon. So far scientists have identified more than sixty meteorites that definitely came from Mars, and they believe the rocks were blasted off the planet's surface by other meteorite impacts. In 2013, data on Mars' atmosphere sent back by the Curiosity rover confirmed that some meteorites really did come from Mars.

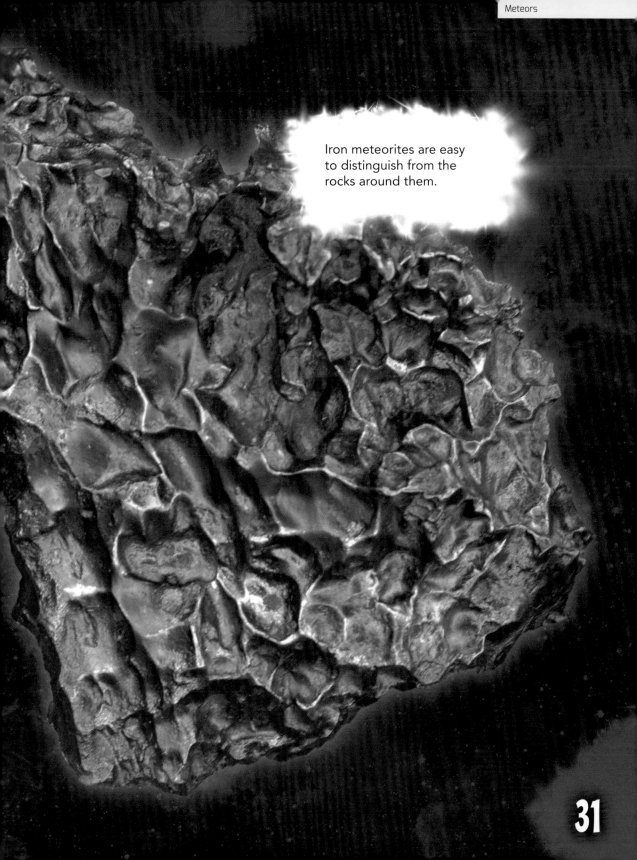

Iron meteorites are easy to distinguish from the rocks around them.

WHAT ELSE IS OUT THERE?

The solar system is home to an incredible range of bodies, from the tiny grains of rock that cause meteors to the giant gas planets orbiting beyond Mars. However, there are many other types of bodies still to explore. One of the most mysterious of these are the centaurs. These elusive objects are small bodies that orbit the sun, mainly between the orbits of Jupiter and Neptune. Their unstable orbits are affected by the gravity of the gas giants, and they sometimes cross the planets' orbits.

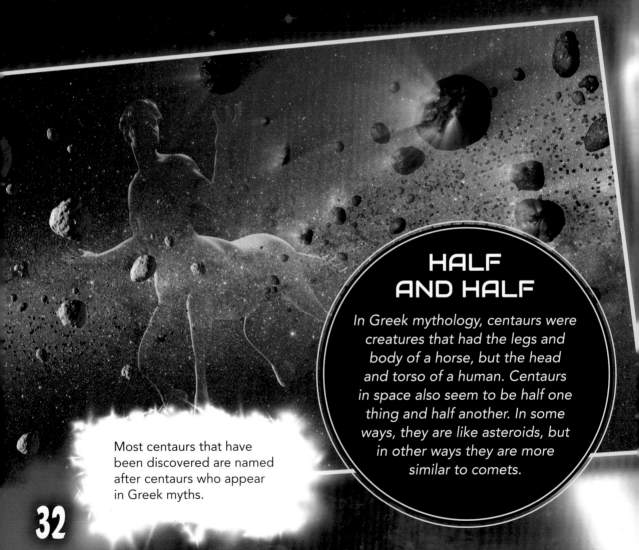

HALF AND HALF

In Greek mythology, centaurs were creatures that had the legs and body of a horse, but the head and torso of a human. Centaurs in space also seem to be half one thing and half another. In some ways, they are like asteroids, but in other ways they are more similar to comets.

Most centaurs that have been discovered are named after centaurs who appear in Greek myths.

Some scientists think that Phoebe, a small moon orbiting Saturn, could be a centaur that was captured by the planet's gravity.

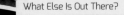

The first centaur, Chiron, was discovered in 1977, and the second, Pholus, in 1992. Since then, hundreds of others have been reported, and astronomers believe that many more are yet to be found. They range in size from tens of miles to about 160 miles (257.5 km) in diameter, which is much larger than most comets. Astronomers believe that most centaurs only spend a relatively short time as centaurs. They will eventually collide with a planet or be thrown by a planet's gravity either toward the sun or out of the solar system.

Some astronomers thought centaurs were asteroids flung out from the inner solar system. Others thought they were comets on their way in from the outer solar system. In 2013, data from NASA's WISE telescope suggested that about two-thirds of centaurs are actually comets. It studied the objects' reflectivity and discovered that most of them are dark, like comets. This means they are probably made from the same materials as a comet. They may have been active comets in the past, and they may be active again one day.

Dwarf Planets

Astronomy is exciting because there are always new developments and discoveries. As technology improves, we learn more about the solar system and the rest of space. Sometimes what we find makes us reevaluate what we thought we knew. This is why, in 2006, the International Astronomical Union (IAU) adopted a new class of space objects: the dwarf planet.

Pluto was discovered in 1930, becoming the ninth planet of the solar system. As astronomers learned more about it, it began to seem like the odd one out among the planets. It was tiny, with an unusual orbit, and was icier than the other rocky planets. In the 1990s, astronomers started finding more objects in the same region of space as Pluto, or even farther away.

By 2005, there were three objects (Quaoar, Eris, and Sedna) that were of a similar size to Pluto. This left astronomers with a problem. Were these new objects also planets? It was likely that several more similar objects were still to be found. How many planets would we end up with? If they were not planets, then where did that leave Pluto?

After a lot of debate, the IAU adopted a new definition of a planet, and created a new category for dwarf planets. Pluto is now called a dwarf planet, along with Ceres, Haumea, Makemake, and Eris. All of these except for Ceres, which is in the asteroid belt, are found in the outer solar system. Several other objects appear to have the characteristics of dwarf planets but have not yet been officially classified. These include Quaoar, Sedna, Salacia, and Orcus.

WHAT IS A PLANET?

Since 2006, the IAU's definition of a planet is that it must orbit the sun, be massive enough to have a nearly round shape, and it must have "cleared the neighborhood" around its orbit. This last requirement means that a planet must be massive enough for its gravity to have removed any smaller rocky or icy objects from its orbit. Objects that meet the first two criteria, but not the third, are now known as dwarf planets.

This illustration shows Pluto and Charon, seen from the surface of one of its smaller moons.

Kuiper Belt Objects

Although Pluto is a long way from the sun, it has a lot of company in the space beyond the orbit of Neptune. It is part of a region called the Kuiper Belt, a flat ring of small icy bodies that orbit the sun. Astronomers estimate that there are hundreds of millions of objects in the Kuiper Belt, most of them left over from the formation of the outer planets.

In the 1950s, the Dutch astronomer Jan Oort (1900–1992) had proposed the existence of a giant spherical cloud of icy bodies, where long-period comets came from. This area is now known as the Oort Cloud. However, another astronomer, Gerard Kuiper (1905–1973), soon realized that short-period comets must come from somewhere closer than the Oort Cloud. He suggested that there was a flattened ring of objects outside the orbit of Neptune. His theory was widely accepted, but it was only in the 1990s that telescopes became powerful and sensitive enough to detect the Kuiper Belt.

In addition to theorizing about the belt that is now named after him, Gerard Kuiper also discovered Uranus's moon Miranda and Neptune's moon Nereid.

Many astronomers believe that Neptune's moon Triton is a captured Kuiper Belt object (KBO).

The first KBO was detected in 1992. Others soon followed, and within twenty years about 1,500 had been identified. Most of the objects that have been detected are fairly large, with diameters between three hundred and one thousand miles (482 and 1,600 km). However, there are likely to be countless smaller objects that are too difficult to make out from Earth. Some of the largest KBOs, including Eris and Pluto, have their own moons. Most KBOs are made mainly of ices, such as methane, ammonia, and water ice. These ices would vaporize if a KBO traveled on a path toward the sun and warmed up, forming a coma and tail.

STUDYING THE KUIPER BELT

In early 2006, when Pluto was still considered to be a planet, the New Horizons spacecraft blasted off from Cape Canaveral in Florida. It is on its way to the Kuiper Belt, where it will become the first spacecraft to visit Pluto and its largest moon, Charon. New Horizons will also attempt to visit one or two other KBOs.

Chapter Six

LOOKING TO
THE FUTURE

There are many reasons for studying smaller solar system bodies such as asteroids, comets, and dwarf planets. They can tell us a lot about how the solar system was formed, and give us clues to the early days of Earth. Asteroids are debris left over from the very early days of the solar system, when the planets were first forming. Their composition can teach us about the elements involved in the chemical mixture that formed Earth.

Asteroids and comets have collided with Earth countless times in the past, and will likely do so again in the future. Finding and tracking objects in space that could one day crash into our planet is an extremely important job. With enough warning, we may be able to take steps to avoid a collision. The more we know about their composition and movement through space, the better prepared we can be.

In the past, the collisions have sometimes had catastrophic effects for life on Earth, but even farther back, they may have helped to create it. Many astronomers believe that the water and organic molecules necessary for life to begin may have arrived on our planet when comets or asteroids crashed into it. Learning more about comets and asteroids could help solve the mystery of how life evolved on Earth.

Telescopes on Earth have provided many key discoveries about the smaller objects in the solar system.

Many writers and movie-makers have imagined what would happen if a large asteroid or comet collided with Earth.

HOW CROWDED IS SPACE?

In movies, the asteroid belt is usually shown as being full of rocks, with spacecraft swerving to avoid collisions. Unfortunately, the reality is much less exciting! As a very rough average, there is about one asteroid within an area the size of Rhode Island. A patch of the asteroid belt the size of the entire United States would have only about two thousand asteroids. If you were standing on an asteroid, the nearest 0.6-mile (1-km) across asteroid would probably be impossible to see without a telescope.

Studying asteroids could help to identify which ones contain useful materials. Some asteroids contain water, precious metals, and phosphorus, all of which can be sent to Earth, or could be used by people on space missions. The asteroids themselves could also be useful as bases for further space exploration.

39

Where Did We Come From?

When Earth first formed about 4.5 billion years ago, it was a very different place from the planet we know now. Its hot surface was constantly changing due to volcanic activity and impacts from meteorites. Eventually things cooled down a little, the surface solidified, and oceans covered much of Earth. At some point about 3.8 billion years ago, the first life appeared on Earth, in the form of single-celled organisms, such as bacteria.

A huge amount of Earth's surface is covered with water, and scientists still disagree on where it all came from.

FILLING THE OCEANS

During the period when Earth was bombarded by asteroids and comets, it would have been very hot, and the oceans would have vaporized. So where did our planet get all its water? One theory is that it came from comets, which are mainly made of ice. Not all comets have the same type of water that is found on Earth, but in 2010, the Deep Impact spacecraft found Earth ocean-type water in Comet Hartley 2.

These pieces of a meteorite fell in California in 2012. Scientists are analyzing the meteorite to learn more about the organic compounds that it contains.

The tiniest unit of life is the cell, and cells themselves are made up of atoms and molecules of a range of different elements. Many scientists believe that living things developed from molecules that could replicate, or make copies of, themselves. Eventually these molecules joined with others, becoming more and more complex. Through the process of evolution, they developed into the wide range of living things we know today.

How those first molecules came about is a subject of much debate. For example, one theory concerns amino acids, some of the building blocks of life. In the 1950s, scientists showed that amino acids could have formed naturally in the early Earth's atmosphere. The necessary raw materials were present, and by using electric sparks to simulate lightning strikes they were able to create amino acids. However, other scientists believe that the building blocks of life could have come from elsewhere in the solar system, brought here on one of the comets or asteroids that crashed into the planet. New discoveries about these objects bring us closer to discovering the truth.

Mining Asteroids

Many of Earth's natural resources are finite. We are using up the available supplies of oil, natural gas, helium, and many other substances. Amazingly, the solution may lie in space: in the near future, we may be able to mine asteroids. Astronomers are already able to use spectroscopy, which analyzes the light reflected from an asteroid, to find out what substances it contains. We know that many asteroids contain iron, nickel, and magnesium. Some could also contain water, oxygen, gold, and platinum.

There are two main reasons for mining asteroids. The first would be to send valuable materials, such as gold and platinum, back to Earth. A second reason would be to extract materials that could help support the astronauts doing the mining, as well as colonies elsewhere in the solar system. For example, extracting water ice would yield water that the colonists could use for drinking and growing food, and it could also be broken down into hydrogen and oxygen to make fuel for rockets. Even the high cost of setting up a mine on an asteroid would probably still be cheaper than sending the same materials from Earth to the moon or Mars.

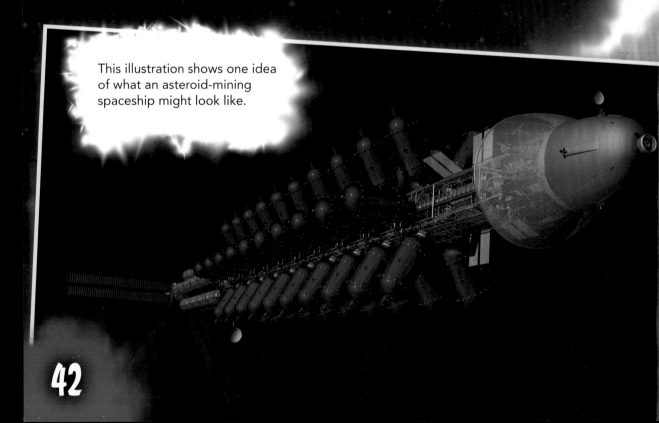

This illustration shows one idea of what an asteroid-mining spaceship might look like.

The theory that many asteroids contain precious metals such as gold has created a lot of interest in the potential of mining them.

An asteroid-mining operation would probably rely heavily on robots, and most machines would be solar powered. Since asteroids have almost no gravity, the astronauts and the mining equipment would have to be anchored to the ground somehow. It would be a challenge, but it could really be worth it: one NASA report estimates that the total amount of minerals found in the asteroid belt would be worth the equivalent of $100 billion for each person living on Earth today!

SPECIAL DELIVERY

Some of the minerals that we already mine from Earth's crust, such as cobalt, platinum, and tungsten, may have originally come from asteroids that collided with Earth. When Earth first formed, it pulled these heavier elements out of the crust and into its core. Scientists believe that asteroids crashing into Earth's crust brought new supplies of these heavy minerals.

43

What's Next?

In the past fifty years, we have learned a huge amount about asteroids, comets, and other small bodies in space. Space agencies such as NASA, ESA, and JAXA are working on future missions to learn more about asteroids and comets. Private companies are getting in on the action, too. One company, Planetary Resources, plans to develop technologies for mining asteroids.

One proposed mission would send astronauts to visit an NEA. It would be a challenging and dangerous mission lasting about six months. The astronauts would be traveling beyond the safety of Earth's magnetic field, leaving them exposed to strong radiation. They would also be too far from Earth for rescue, if anything went wrong.

However, one safer option for studying asteroids up close would be to use a robotic spacecraft to drag a small asteroid into orbit around the moon. From there, it would be easier to study or to mine. NASA scientists believe that such a mission would be possible in the near future. One plan would use a slow-moving spacecraft with a large bag to catch an asteroid about twenty feet (6 m) across, then drag it to the moon.

This illustration shows just one of several ideas for technologies to capture an asteroid.

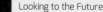

OSIRIS-REx will take three years to reach the asteroid, and will study it for more than a year.

WHAT'S THE POINT?

Capturing an asteroid sounds fascinating, but is there enough of a reason to do it? It would provide an opportunity for us to test out techniques that would allow us to send manned missions to NEAs. It could also be a chance to test mining techniques and see for certain what kinds of materials can be extracted. It would be a way of testing technologies for controlling or deflecting asteroids on a course to collide with Earth.

Other missions are already in progress. NASA's OSIRIS-REx spacecraft will launch soon and will study and map the surface of an asteroid called Bennu, then return a sample of its rock to Earth. Scientists hope that the material will provide clues into the origin of life on Earth, and also the possibility of life elsewhere in the solar system.

GLOSSARY

amino acids Organic chemicals necessary to build proteins.

asteroids Small, rocky bodies that orbit the sun.

atmosphere The layer of gases surrounding a planet or moon.

atoms The smallest possible units of a chemical element. Atoms are the basis of all matter in the universe.

cell The smallest unit of life.

centaurs Small objects in the solar system that have some characteristics of comets and some characteristics of asteroids.

coma The glowing cloud that surrounds the nucleus of a comet when it is close to the sun.

comets Icy objects in space that travel in long, looping paths around the sun.

crater A hollow area, like the inside of a bowl, created when an object crashes into a planet or other large object.

crust The hard outer shell of something.

dwarf planet An object in the solar system that has not cleared out its own orbit of other major bodies in order to be considered a planet.

fireball An exceptionally bright meteor.

galaxies Groups of hundreds of billions of stars and other matter held together by gravity.

gravity The force that pulls all objects toward each other.

infrared A type of electromagnetic energy with a long wavelength, which cannot be seen as visible light.

ion drive A type of engine that uses charged particles to provide thrust.

mantle The part of a planet, asteroid, or comet that lies between the crust and the central core.

meteorites Lumps of stone or metal from a meteor that has landed on Earth.

meteoroids Small lumps of rock or other matter that travel through the solar system.

meteors The bright streaks in the sky seen when meteoroids travel through Earth's atmosphere.

meteor shower An event when many meteors appear in the sky, appearing to come from the same source.

molecules The smallest units of substances that have all the properties of those substances. Molecules are made up of atoms.

natural resources Materials that are found in nature and that can be used by people in many ways.

nucleus The central part of a comet, which vaporizes when it nears the sun to produce a coma and tail.

orbiting When one body in space travels on a curved path around another object, such as a moon orbiting a planet.

probe An instrument or tool used to explore something that cannot be observed directly.

protoplanets Objects in space that are planets in their early stages of evolution.

radiation Waves of energy sent out by sources of heat or light, such as the sun. Radiation can be harmful to living things.

rotated Spun around a central axis. The rotation of Earth is what causes night and day.

trojans Rocky objects in space that share the orbit of a much larger object, such as a planet.

vaporize To turn into gas.

FOR MORE INFORMATION

Books

Aguilar, David A. *Space Encyclopedia: A Tour of Our Solar System and Beyond*. Washington, D.C.: National Geographic Kids, 2013.

Atkinson, Stuart. *Comets, Asteroids, and Meteors* (Astronaut Travel Guides). Chicago, IL: Heinemann-Raintree, 2013.

Carson, Mary Kay. *Far-Out Guide to Asteroids and Comets* (Far-Out Guide to the Solar System). Berkeley Heights, NJ: Enslow Publishers, 2013.

Einspruch, Andrew. *Mysteries of the Universe: How Astronomers Explore Space* (National Geographic Science Chapters). Washington, D.C.: National Geographic Children's Books, 2006.

Simon, Seymour. *Our Solar System*. New York, NY: HarperCollins, 2014.

Websites

Due to the changing nature of Internet links, Rosen Publishing has developed an online list of websites related to the subject of this book. This site is updated regularly. Please use this link to access the list:

http://www.rosenlinks.com/SSS/Comet

INDEX